# Living on Purpose
## *Designing a Life You Love*

# Table of Contents

The purpose of life is not to be happy. It is to be useful, to be honorable, to be compassionate, to have it make some difference that you have lived and lived well.

— Ralph Waldo Emerson

# Chapter 1. Introduction

Discover the magic of living with intent in our Special Report: "Living on Purpose: Designing a Life You Love." Uncover true joy and fulfillment by designing your life around what truly matters to you. There are no technicalities here, only rich, life-changing insights to guide you on your journey. Learn from experts' testament and strategies that will bring sparkle, vitality, and a profound sense of purpose to your every day. Immerse yourself in this extraordinary guide, and you'll be astonished at the transformation that ensues. Trust us; this electrifying report is much more than words on paper—it's the first step in forming the life you've always dreamt of. Dare to live a life on purpose, dare to design a life you love! Start today, begin with this report. Your exciting journey of self-discovery and fulfillment awaits!

# Chapter 2. Defining Your Life's Purpose: The Compass Pointing to Fulfillment

Imagine clutching a compass in your hand, its magnetic needle steadying after a brief whirl, finally pointing you in a specific direction. Life purpose functions in a strikingly similar way. Like that little magnetized needle in a compass, your life's purpose gives you direction, aligning your actions and decisions to the things that truly matter. In this chapter, we unravel how to define your life's purpose – the compass pointing towards fulfillment.

## 2.1. Identifying Your Natural Inclinations and Interests

The first step in defining your life's purpose is identifying your natural inclinations and interests. What kind of activities do you find engaging? What topics can hold your attention effortlessly? Reflective exercises, journaling, and meditation can help to deepen your understanding. Delving into your inclinations and interests forms the foundation of purpose identification. As you excavate these hidden treasures, you begin to understand yourself in a more lucid, coherent, and fulfilling manner.

## 2.2. Examining Your Skills and Talents

In the second step, we explore your unique skills and talents. Everyone is gifted with a unique combination of skills and talents. Understanding them and aligning them with your natural inclinations and interests can add significant momentum in your journey towards fulfilling your life purpose. Consider taking psychometric tests or working with a career coach to discern your core competencies. Be sure to also reflect on feedback from friends, family, teachers, mentors, and colleagues.

## 2.3. Taking Stock of Your Achievements

Next, capturing a list of your achievements and success stories paves the way in discovering your life's purpose. Ask yourself, in what aspects of your life have you genuinely felt successful or accomplished? What opportunities have left you more enriched, personally and professionally? Assessing your achievements provides touchpoints of fulfillment and success, informing your pursuit of purpose.

## 2.4. Visualizing Your Ideal Self

By this stage, you have a firm grasp of your interests, skills, and achievements. The next step is to envision your ideal self. Imagine that all limitations have evaporated and you are living your best life. What does it look like? What is your role in this life? What are you accomplishing? Who are you working with, and what impacts are you making? Understanding your ideal self creates a powerful mental blueprint of the life that you would love to live, steering you closer to your purpose.

## 2.5. Drafting Your Purpose Statement

Equipped with all these insights, words, thoughts, feelings, reflections, you are now ready to draft your personal purpose statement. It's a declaration that encapsulates your life's purpose, serving as a reminder and guide in your journey. It can be as short as a sentence or as long as a paragraph; the critical aspect is its precision and its alignment with your true self.

# 2.6. Aligning Your Purpose with Your Actions

Finally, define strategies and concrete steps to align your life's purpose with your day-to-day actions. This alignment is crucial in creating a life by design rather than by default. Breaking down your purpose into smaller, manageable goals will not only ensure that your purpose becomes an inherent part of your lifestyle, but it will also make the journey towards fulfillment more attainable and enjoyable.

Remember always, your life's purpose is not a fixed destination but a continually evolving guide. As you grow and change, allow your purpose to morph and adapt. Designing a meaningful life around your purpose involves constant reflection and agility. Embrace the transformative power of purpose as your personal compass to fulfillment, leading you towards the life you've always dreamt of. The magic of purposeful living awaits! This is an invitation to let your life's purpose be your guiding compass—it's your journey, take the first step today.

# Chapter 3. Identifying Your Core Values: The Building Blocks of Purposeful Living

In this journey towards a life lived with purpose, one initial and significant step is to understand fully, acknowledge, and articulate your core values. These tenets serve as the building blocks of intentional and purposeful living. They are the essence of who we truly are, dictating our actions, shaping our reactions, and influencing our decisions both consciously and subconsciously. Let us delve deeper into the concept of core values and their power in assisting us to live a life of authenticity, fulfillment, and purpose.

## 3.1. Laying the Groundwork: What Are Core Values?

To put it simply, core values are the central principles that govern our lives. They represent the ethos we hold dear, the beliefs we steadfastly adhere to, and the conduct we aim to embody. They are, in essence, our moral compass, quietly directing us as we navigate the vast ocean of life. They are ingrained in the deepest recesses of our beings, often so entrenched that we may not even consciously be aware of them.

Core values are not fleeting passions, whims, or desires. They are not influenced by external environment or trends. Rather, they are enduring and constant, able to weather the harshest storms and emerge unscathed. They shape our identity and form the backbone of our character.

Understanding our core values gives us a profound insight into our true selves, allowing us to lead lives that resonates with who we fundamentally are. Recognizing these pivotal cornerstones of our identity serves as an imperative step towards a purposeful life.

## 3.2. The Importance of Identifying Core Values

Identifying core values forms the foundation of life lived with purpose. Not only do they provide a moral compass, guiding our decisions both large and small, but they also offer a sense of clarity and direct our actions. They form the yardstick against which we evaluate ourselves and our progress in life.

When our actions and decisions align with our core values, there is a sense of contentment and fulfillment due to coherence between our inner selves and outer actions. When they do not, we might experience a gnawing feeling of discord, dissatisfaction or restlessness.

Knowing our core values brings greater clarity to our lives. They enable us to decipher situations and make decisions that reflect our true selves. They become the guiding beacon illuminating our way, even amid the densest fog of uncertainty and indecision.

## 3.3. The Process of Determining Your Core Values

Identifying personal core values is a journey of introspection and self-discovery. It involves delving deep into oneself, questioning beliefs, confronting biases, and relentlessly seeking the truth about who you are at your core.

Start by reflecting on instances when you felt intense satisfaction, pride, or alignment. What were the circumstances? Conversely, consider situations that sparked intense discomfort, disharmony, or anger in you. What factors or values were being compromised or dishonored in these situations?

To assist in this process, make a list of potential core values. These could range from concepts like honesty, community, creativity, love, perseverance, or freedom. Aim for about 15-20 core values. Then, start the process of elimination. Consider each value deeply and try to discern which ones truly align with who you are.

This may be challenging but remember that it isn't a one-time assignment. It requires patience, kindness to oneself, and the willingness to revisit and revise. What you will have at the end of this is a coherent set of core values, a veritable guide to your authentic self.

# 3.4. Living in Alignment with Your Core Values

Once you have identified your core values, the next step is to align these with your daily life. This doesn't happen overnight; it is an ongoing process that requires continuous effort, reassessment, and refinement.

Whether it's choices about your career, relationships, self-care, or lifestyle, ensure that your decisions are in line with your core values. Living in alignment with your core values infuses a sense of authenticity, joy, and fulfillment in your life, making every moment infused with purpose.

Breathe life into your core values by actively embodying them. If creativity is a core value, for instance, express your creativity in your work, hobbies, or self-expression.

# 3.5. Embracing Your Core Values as Your Life's Blueprint

Your core values are more than just words or principles—they should form your life's blueprint, guiding you towards a life of fulfillment and purpose. They serve as the anchor during trying times and provide the impetus to strive, grow, and evolve.

Communicate your core values to those around you. Not only will this enhance your relationships by providing a window into your soul, but it will also attract people with similar beliefs and values, fostering mutual respect and understanding.

Remember, your core values are intrinsic to you - they are not negotiable or open to compromise. They form the edifice upon which a fulfilling and meaningful life can be built. Embrace them, live them, and honor them, and watch as your life unfolds with an unwavering sense of purpose and delight.

In conclusion, identifying your core values is a critical step in designing the life you love. These are the elements that make you genuinely you. Your core values serve as the steadfast sail guiding your ship of purpose, navigating you towards a life lived with intentionality, authenticity, and fulfillment.

# Chapter 4. Designing Your Intent-based Goals: Mapping the Life You Love

To embark on the incredible journey of designing a life around your authentic self, distinguishing your intent-based goals is integral. This chapter is a detailed exploration covering the steps involved in recognising, crafting, and harnessing the power of these intent-based goals.

## 4.1. The Necessity and Power of Intent-based Goals

An intent-based goal is a goal born out of the deepest yearnings of your authentic self. Unlike traditional goals that are often derived from external influences, societal pressures, or perceived notions of success, intent-based goals offer a unified vision that aligns with your core values and life purpose. They serve as the guidance, leading you towards a life you love.

The magic of intent-based goals lies in their inherent ability to empower personal growth, nurture happiness, and engender fulfillment. They act as internal compasses, directing you to sail the vast ocean of life towards your desired horizon. These goals encapsulate your essence, reflect your true desires, and carve the pathway for a life nourished by purpose.

## 4.2. Crafting Your Intent-based Goals

Crafting intent-based goals involve introspection and self-discovery.

It's a poetic infusion of your innermost desires, core values, and life's purpose projected into tangible, achievable goals. Here's a step-by-step guide:

1. Identify your core values and life purpose: Grounded in the lessons from the previous chapters, this step involves revisiting your discovered core values and your defined life's purpose. Write them down and internalise them.

2. Reflect on your desires: In a quiet, uninterrupted space, take a moment to introspect. What are your deepest desires? How do those desires align with your core values and life's purpose? Be patient; allow your thoughts to flow freely.

3. Chart out your goals: Now, transform these desires into tangible goals. Make sure they align with your core values and life's purpose. They should serve as practical guiding tools to lead a life you love.

4. Define the characteristics of each goal: Each goal should be SMART - Specific, Measurable, Achievable, Relevant, Time-bound. Structuring your goals this way provides clarity, and the means to track your progress.

# 4.3. The Art of Nurturing Your Intent-Based Goals

Successful engagement with intent-based goals necessitates personal commitment, self-discipline, and resilience. Embrace these strategies to empower your goals journey:

1. Maintain a written record: Writing your goals catalyses commitment. Revisiting regularly keeps you focused and driven.

2. Visualise achievement: Practice mental imagery of achieving your goals. Feel the abundance of joy and fulfillment. This mental exercise nurtures motivation.

3. Develop an action plan: Design an action plan detailing steps to progress towards your goals. This enhances accountability and provides a navigational guide for your journey.

4. Embrace setbacks: Failure and setbacks are opportunities for growth. Understand, evaluate, and learn from them.

5. Celebrate small wins: Acknowledge and celebrate your small wins. These celebrations foster motivation and a positive mindset.

From their conception to fruition, intent-based goals emerge as fundamental pillars supporting your vision of life. Their power to indispensable in shaping and actualising your cherished life's design. They prompt constructive change, encouraging living daily with conscious intent and deliberate action, suffusing your life with sparkling vitality and profound purpose.

Nestled within these identified and nurtured intent-based goals hides the magic key to designing life the way you love — a life thriving with intent, passion, and purpose. It's your personal passport to a satisfying journey of incredible self-discovery and abundant fulfillment. Embrace it, and chart your course towards that fulfilling life you aspire to, love, and deserve.

# Chapter 5. Overcoming Obstacles: Turning Challenges Into Stepping Stones

In life, it's inevitable to encounter obstacles that may seem daunting and insurmountable. This chapter is dedicated to transforming your perspective about these obstacles, transforming them from roadblocks into stepping stones towards your life's purpose. More than just learning to deal with these hindrances, we shall delve into strategies and perspectives that allow you to turn challenges into growth opportunities.

## 5.1. The Nature of Obstacles

Every individual's pathway contains stumbling blocks, and these often materialize in various guises: physical, psychological, financial, or relational, among others. Regardless of their nature, obstacles have one thing in common—they steer us out of our comfort zone, compelling us to either confront these hurdles or evade them altogether. Embracing the challenges in our lives isn't just about surviving; it's about developing resilience, cultivating wisdom, and harnessing courage. They build character, shaping us into better persons on our journey towards a life lived with intent.

## 5.2. Changing Your Perception About Obstacles

The first vital step in overcoming obstacles is altering our perception concerning challenges. Our perspective plays a colossal role in how we react and negotiate difficulties. Embracing a mind frame that chooses to view obstacles as opportunities increasingly aides in overcoming them. Obstacles often provide a learning experience and an occasion to enhance various life skills. Eventual success becomes increasingly likely when we approach issues with a problem-solving mindset rather than that of a victim. Hence, obstacles begin to transform into stepping stones.

# 5.3. Tactics for Surmounting Difficulties

Tackling life's challenges necessitates tactical maneuvering. Solutions such as reframing the issue, breaking down the problem into manageable portions, and seeking inspirations or learning from others' experiences can be incredibly advantageous in these circumstances. Additionally, maintaining an optimal level of physical and mental wellbeing provides the endurance to cope with trials and tribulations. Furthermore, employing stress management techniques such as meditation, journaling, and engaging in hobbies can provide a breather amidst the chaos, reinstating our calm and focus.

# 5.4. Learn, Persist, and Evolve

Every obstacle provides a lesson—the trick lies in learning those lessons and applying them in our lives. This continuous cycle lends us an opportunity to grow and curve out a niche for ourselves. Identifying the teachings each obstacle carries, persisting on the path of purpose despite skirmishes and evolving from each encounter—these three stages signify the transformation from seeing challenges as hindrances to stepping stones.

# 5.5. The impact of Overcoming Obstacles on Life's Purpose

Every challenge braved contributes to our journey towards our life's purpose. They offer us the opportunity to reassess and reevaluate our intentions, helping us align with our true calling. Overcoming obstacles in the journey of purposeful living absorbs resilience, courage, compassion, and wisdom—traits that don't just morph us into better individuals but also underpin the foundation of a life lived on purpose.

In conclusion, the art of overcoming obstacles correlates heavily with living a life of intent and purpose. Challenges aren't blockades that stall us in our journey but helpful tools that shape us, funnel us towards our true purpose, teaching us valuable lessons in the process. It's about embracing the difficulty, persisting amidst trials, and continually learning and growing. As we learn to navigate these obstacles effectively and with grace, we draw one step closer to designing a life we love. Remember, your journey is unique—do not let hurdles deter you; instead, let them be the stepping stones to your life of purpose, passion, and fulfillment.

# Chapter 6. The Art of Decision Making: The Guiding Principle of Purposeful Life

The vitality of decision making is elusive yet profound, serving as the fulcrum upon which the lever of life balance swings. Its importance touches every corner of our existence, from the smallest everyday details to the grandest, life-altering choices.

## 6.1. The Power of Choice and Consequences

A decision, at its core, is a choice between several options that ultimately generates a particular outcome. Each choice we make is like a spark that ignites a chain reaction. This chain's resultant fire, for better or worse, is what we commonly refer to as consequences.

An accurate understanding of the power of your choices is an important step in mastering the art of decision making. Each decision, no matter how trivial it may seem, holds potential. It's like a minor directional adjustment during a long journey—over time, it can lead to a significantly different destination.

The intertwining complexity of decisions and the subsequent ripple effects they generate shape the trajectory of our lives. To embrace life with intent and navigate our journey with deliberate purpose, we must understand, respect, and wield this potent power.

# 6.2. Decision Making and Core Values

In the context of a purposeful life, your decision making should align with your core values and life's purpose. Like a compass guiding sailors across ocean expanses, your values steer your decisions amidst the turbulent waves of life.

Adherence to your core values in decision making creates harmony with the life you desire. Whether you're deciding on a career path, a relationship, or simply how to spend your day, your core values serve as guiding posts that keep you aligned with your purpose.

# 6.3. The Decision Making Process

The process of decision making, while it may seem intuitive, benefits greatly from a structured approach. A systematic process injects a measure of objectivity into what could otherwise become an emotional whirlwind. This is especially true for vital decisions that have a significant impact on your life.

Decision making generally involves identifying the problem or decision to be made, gathering relevant information, identifying possible options, evaluating these alternatives, making the selection, and finally, implementing and reviewing the decision.

# 6.4. A Rational Approach to Decisions

A rational, methodical approach is often considered the gold standard of decision making. It encourages objectivity, fosters clarity, and discourages rash, impulsive choices. The rational decision-making process typically involves:

1. Defining the problem or decision

2. Gathering and evaluating relevant information

3. Identifying possible solutions or courses of action

4. Evaluating these alternatives based on defined criteria

5. Making the decision

6. Implementing the chosen decision

7. Reviewing the decision and its outcomes

This rational model, however, is not free from criticisms. Its applicability often diminishes in complex, real-world situations that involve uncertainty, ambiguous information, and shifting goalposts.

# 6.5. Emotional Intelligence and Decision Making

When confronted with situations that challenge the conventional rational model, emotional intelligence plays a crucial role. It provides the ability to manage emotions, to perceive and interpret others' emotions, and to utilize this emotional information in decision making.

Emotional intelligence mitigates the limitations of purely rational decision-making approaches. It takes into account subjective experiences and human responses that are at once complex, nuanced, and profoundly human.

# 6.6. Mindfulness and Decision Making

Mindfulness, the practice of focusing one's awareness on the present moment, also plays a critical role in effective decision making. It reduces impulsivity and fosters a clear, focused mind, enabling more balanced decisions.

Mindfulness builds a strong foundation for a purposeful life, inculcating a keen awareness of your everyday decisions and their alignment with your life's purpose.

# 6.7. Decision Fatigue: A Threat to Purposeful Decision Making

Decision fatigue is a common, yet often unrecognized, threat to purposeful decision making. It refers to the degradation of the quality of one's decisions after a long session of decision making. This phenomenon underscores the importance of deliberate, meaningful rest and its role in maintaining resilient, high-quality decision-making capabilities.

In conclusion, the art of decision making is a pivotal facet of living a purposeful life. Mastering this art requires understanding the dynamic interplay of rational thought, emotional intelligence, and mindfulness. By grasping the significance of each decision you make and aligning it with your core values and purpose, you're on your way to a life well-designed—a life you love.

# Chapter 7. Cultivating Positive Habits: Your Daily Dose of Purposeful Actions

The journey towards a purposeful life is intrinsically tied to the continuous activity of cultivating positive habits. We all find ourselves bending towards certain patterns and behaviours, they are the scripted roadmaps that define our everyday life. Positive habits, however, are not adopted casually or by chance, they are consciously plucked up from the garden of potential behaviours and cultivated until they bear fruitful results. This laborious process of ingraining a positive habit takes an understanding of how habits form, the ability to identify which habits augment our purpose, and the willpower to sustainably embed them in the rhythms of our daily routines.

## 7.1. Understanding and Utilizing the Habit Loop

At the heart of developing a habit lies the understanding of the 'Habit Loop' - a three-part cycle that governs how habits form and operate. It comprises a cue or trigger, a routine or action, and a reward. The cue signals the brain to go into auto-pilot mode and enables a particular habit. The routine is the actual behaviour or action, while the reward is the positive feeling or benefit gained from executing the habit.

Recognizing this loop can allow you to deconstruct your existing habits and 'hack' them to develop positive ones. Interlace the positive habit you want to cultivate within this loop. Identify a suitable cue, perform the action, and give yourself some form of rewarding reinforcement. Over time, this cycle will solidify into an automatic behaviour, a positive habit.

# 7.2. Recognizing Your Purpose-Aiding Habits

Your purpose does not survive in a vacuum; it thrives when fortified by a series of purpose-adherent habits or actions. Recognizing these habits starts with understanding the contours of your purpose. Once you understand your life's guiding ethos, you can dissect it into different facets and identify actions that catalyze each facet.

For instance, if your purpose involves spreading kindness, a suitable habit could be practicing daily acts of generosity. If your purpose lies in health and wellness, a habit could be preparing nutritious meals or regular exercise. Remember that each habit, while small in itself, contributes to the larger framework and vision of your purpose.

# 7.3. Integrating Positive Habits into Daily Routines

Any habit, to cement itself, needs to symmetrically fit into the puzzle of your daily life. Cherishing your positive habits requires placing them within the framework of your everyday routines. Ingredient one involves conscious effort, where the action is deliberately undertaken and consistently reminded. Gradually, ingredient two, habituation, takes over, making the action a natural, almost instinctive, part of your day.

For successful integration, you could attach a new habit to an existing routine. This technique, often called 'habit stacking' uses the habitual nature of an existing habit to cue and reinforce a new habit.

# 7.4. Sustaining Purposeful Habits over Time

The essence of a habit lies in its consistency and sustainability over time. It is indeed a marathon and not a sprint. You should be kind to yourself, allow for setbacks, and focus on gradual improvement rather than immediate perfection.

Log your progress, celebrate small victories, and allow lessons from occasional missteps to guide future actions. Remember, evolving and nurturing positive habits is a lifelong journey, a continuous conversation between your everyday actions and your larger life purpose.

# 7.5. Collaborative Habit Development

Lastly, as you carve this path towards purposeful living, you need not walk alone. Positive habits can also flourish through collective nurturing and collaborative efforts. Engage with loved ones, find accountability partners, or join communities of shared interest. These platforms can provide motivation, offer constructive critique, and infuse a sense of camaraderie in your journey.

Cultivating positive habits, then, is not a sudden alteration but a painstaking and thoughtful process. It involves distinguishing what habits serve our purpose from what does not and consciously integrating these into our lives. Remember, our daily habits are the threads that weave the grand tapestry of purposeful life. Let them be woven with intention, consistency, and love.

# Chapter 8. Balancing Your Life: Ensuring All Areas Flourish in Sync

A balanced life is not just a lofty ideal, but a tangible, achievable reality. Life, in all its various facets – work, relationships, personal growth – should flourish like a luxuriant garden, each aspect cared for and nurtured in sync with others, ensuring overall well-being and fulfillment. This journey of balancing your life will be astutely navigated in this section, with each nuance, each thread of thought and action woven intricately to guide you towards the design of a life you love.

## 8.1. Understanding Life Balance

The concept of life balance is comparable to the delicate equilibrium maintained by a skilled tightrope walker, where too much weight on one side can result in a catastrophic fall. Like that tightrope walker, we must maintain a careful balance between the various compartments of our life if we hope to achieve overall satisfaction and contentment. Life balance isn't just a static state of nirvana, but rather a dynamic process of constant adjustment, self-correction, and adaptation, akin to a continuous dance of integration and flux.

## 8.2. The Dimensions of a Balanced Life

When we think of the elements that make up a well-rounded life, the categories that pop into our minds typically include work or profession, personal growth, health, relationships, recreation, and spiritual progress. Each of these dimensions require attention, effort, and the judicious allocation of our time and energy, requiring us to periodically reassess and realign our priorities to ensure an harmonious existence.

# 8.3. Strategies for Life Balance

Achieving equilibrium in life is a practice that necessitates purposeful intent and focused effort. The following practical strategies offer a roadmap to maintaining balance across all your life's dimensions:

1. **Prioritize And Set Boundaries**: Delineate the most pivotal parts of your life and assign time dedicatedly to them. Set boundaries to prevent one aspect of your life from encroaching on the others.

2. **Nurture Relationships**: Allocate time and energy to fostering healthy connections with loved ones – family, friends, and community.

3. **Invest in Personal Growth**: A balanced life necessitates continuous learning and growth. Commit time each day to educate yourself, acquire new skills, and intellectually evolve.

4. **Foster a Healthy Lifestyle**: Prioritize your physical health through regular exercise, balanced nutrition, and sufficient sleep. Also, ensure to devote time to activities that refresh your mind and rejuvenate your spirit.

5. **Time for Leisure**: Life isn't all about seriousness. Make sure to include recreational activities that you enjoy for leisure and relaxation.

6. **Practice Mindfulness**: Stay in the present moment, savoring every experience, without anxiously fretting about the future or ruefully regretting the past.

7. **Spiritual Nourishment**: Many find solace and tranquility in spirituality. If this rings true for you, make sure to reserve time for prayer, meditation, or any practice that helps you connect

with the divine.

## 8.4. Embracing the Cycle of Self-Correction

Our life balance is not a "set-it-and-forget-it" venture. Instead, life demands that we remain flexible and open to constant adaptation and change. And it's here lies the wonder of self-correction - the ability to adapt, tweak, and realign our steps as we dance through life's trials and tribulations. Recognizing when we have strayed off our chosen path, and possessing the courage and resolve to steer ourselves back, is central to maintaining harmony in our lives.

## 8.5. The Implication of Balance on Life Design

A balanced life assures you of a holistic impact across all facets, fostering joy and fulfillment in each one, and promoting overall wellbeing. When you design your life with a concentration on balance, you allow yourself the space to grow, learn, love, and contribute positively to the world around you. This underscores the importance of collaboration between all the individual aspects of your life, rather than championing one single domain.

This deliberate dialogue of balance seizes you by the hand, steering you clear of turbulent oceans, guiding you along safe harbors. It provides you with the bedrock on which to erect the edifice of your grand design – a life you passionately love!

To sum up, the keen pursuit of balance in one's life is not an optional endeavor, but a critical element in the quest towards designing a life imbued with authentic purpose. It is a dance—a delightful blend of ebb and flow, give and take, work and play — that bursts forth with a vibrancy, sparkle, and vitality unique to you. Crafting a balanced life, appointed with ample nourishment for every facet, bestows a profound sense of existential fulfillment, contributing to the magical adventure of living life on purpose. Never underestimate the transformative power of a balanced life. You have all the potential to make it happen – start today, start now!

# Chapter 9. Resilience and Adaptability: Thriving Amid Uncertainty

In an everchanging world marked by rapid technological advancements and ceaseless societal transformations, our ability to resiliently adapt to uncertainty becomes a cornerstone for building a purposeful life. This chapter aims to guide you towards understanding and honing this crucial skill set of resilience and adaptability.

## 9.1. The Rationale for Resilience

First and foremost, let's delve into understanding resilience. Resilience is often compared to a rubber band's quality to regain its original shape after being stretched by stress and pressure. In life, resilience is the ability to recover from adversities, only to emerge stronger and more determined.

Resilience is the emotional strength that fortifies us to face life's trials. From significant life changes to daily stresses, a resilient individual can navigate through tough times while maintaining their mental health. The importance of resilience in our lives is manifold. It helps us to accept our past, endure the present, and anticipate our future – but with a refreshing sense of optimism and hope. For a life of purpose, resilience is undoubtedly an essential attribute.

## 9.2. The Power of Adaptability

Complementing resilience, we have adaptability. Yet another critical life competency, adaptability refers to an individual's capacity to modify or change their thoughts, actions, and feelings to cope with change or unfamiliar situations effectively.

Our capability to adapt is the oil in our life's engine that allows us to maintain a smooth ride despite the road's unpredictable bumps and bends. From embracing technological innovation to adjusting to new environments, adaptability enables us to maintain our focus, perspective, and fulfillment amidst uncertainty.

# 9.3. Cultivating Resilience and Adaptability

Now that we've defined and understood the significance of resilience and adaptability, let's explore practical strategies on how to cultivate these beleaguered skills. You weren't born with fixed quantities of resilience and adaptability. Instead, these dynamic qualities can be developed over time, much like a muscle that strengthens through exercise.

1. Seek for Progress, Not Perfection: Shifting your focus from absolute perfection to constant progress can help boost your resilience while promoting adaptability. Celebrate small victories as each success fuels your confidence to deal with bigger challenges.

2. Maintain a Positive Attitude: A positive attitude is the lifeblood of resilience. Cultivate optimism and gratitude in your day-to-day life. Practice reframing negative thoughts and focusing on possibilities instead of problems.

3. Embrace Change: Adapting to change is the very key to adaptability. Open up to new experiences, new ideas, and new ways of living. Remember; change is often the door leading to growth.

4. Seek Support: Building a network of supportive, positive individuals can significantly buffer stress and help build resilience. Engage in meaningful interactions and foster relations

that encourage strength and growth.

# 9.4. Resilience and Adaptability in Action: Real-Life Examples

Examining real-life scenarios where resilience and adaptability were employed successfully can provide inspiration and practical lessons. Here, we will discuss a few such instances. Remember, the stories of individuals overcoming hardships and embracing change are never too far from our reach; be it in popular literature, history, or even within our own community or family.

The principle is that build up of resilience and adaptability can unlock a world of possibilities, allowing us to thrive amidst uncertainty and effectively map a purposeful life amidst all odds.

# 9.5. Nourishing Resilience and Adaptability: The Ongoing Journey

Remember, cultivating resilience and adaptability isn't a one-time task. It is an ongoing journey that requires continuous effort. Show compassion towards yourself, maintain your sense of humor, and never hesitate to seek help when needed. The process may seem demanding, but the outcome—a life marked by intensities of joy, purpose, and fulfillment—is well worth the endeavor.

With each setback and each change, remember to call upon your resilience and adaptability. They are there to protect and guide you, to help you emerge stronger and wiser. And it's from this foundation of resilience and adaptability that you can truly start to design and live a life you love.

In the face of uncertainty and inevitable change, resilience and adaptability become defining factors on our journey to design a life of purpose and fulfillment. This journey towards a resilient and adaptable self is arduous yet ultimately rewarding. The process deepens our understanding of self, enriches our life experiences, and strengthens our capacities to live a life that embodies our deepest core values and life goals. Hence, cultivating resilience and adaptability is not merely a desirable trait; it is a requisite for those who dare to live a life on purpose, a life they truly love!

# Chapter 10. Building a Supportive Community: Crucial Allies in Your Journey of Life Design

An often overlooked aspect of personal growth, self-realization, and designing a life of intent is the surrounding environment, and more specifically, the people who inhabit it. The ties we bind with others remarkably impact our beliefs, attitudes, motivation, and actions, ultimately influencing our journey towards a purposeful life. By thoughtfully constructing a supportive community around us, we create a nurturing environment that cultivates our individual values and enlivens the spirit of living with intent.

## 10.1. The Value of Supportive Relationships

For much of history, humans have relied on community for survival. This primal need for social interaction has transformed over time, with contemporary society prioritizing the emotional needs and psychological health derived from relationships. Research has demonstrated a strong correlation between supportive interpersonal relationships and improved wellbeing, lower stress levels, increased self-esteem, and a general sense of fulfillment.

It's not just about having numerous friends or a large family, but about the quality of those relationships. Beyond mere companionship, relationships should foster a sense of understanding, acceptance, encouragement, and inspiration. In the voyage to a life designed intentionally and authentically, the emotional buoyancy provided by a supportive community is invaluable.

# 10.2. Identifying Supportive Individuals

Who are these supportive individuals that could stand as crucial allies in your journey? They are the cheerleaders who celebrate your achievements and compassionately understand your challenges. They are mentors with wisdom to impart and listeners eager to understand.

Start by examining your current social circles and identifying who positively influences your life. Who encourages you to be your best self? Who listens with empathy, offers constructive criticism, and respects your values? Once you have an understanding of the qualities that constitute a supportive individual, you can better cultivate and maintain such relationships.

# 10.3. Cultivating a Supportive Community

Building a robust and supportive community requires purposeful effort. In many ways, it mirrors the journey of self-discovery and life design: it demands honesty, patience, and persistence.

The first step involves reaching out and connecting with others who share similar values or aspirations. Attend local gatherings, join clubs, volunteer, or become active in online communities. While it can feel daunting or uncomfortable, initial discomfort often leads to enriched personal connections.

It's equally important to invest time and emotional energy in current relationships that promote growth and offer mutual support. Keep open lines of communication, engage meaningfully, and show appreciation. Remember, reciprocity is vital; you also have to be a supportive friend, mentor, or family member. Exude empathy, show kindness, and inspire others as they have inspired you.

# 10.4. Thriving Together

Creating a supportive community is more than just a backbone for personal growth; it enables collective growth. Shared experiences and diverse perspectives encourage learning and development, fostering a shared sense of purpose and contributing to an enriching life design.

Life's challenges might seem more manageable when navigation occurs within a supportive community. These networks serve as rallying forces during turbulent periods, providing comfort, advice, and sometimes just the simple, heartening presence of comradeship.

Building a supportive community is an essential pillar in the architecture of a purpose-filled life. The interwoven relationships not only promote personal growth and resilience but also form a treasured part of our human experience. And as you continue your journey of intent, remember that this task isn't a solitary endeavor. You will be sharing, exerting, learning, and growing in concert with others—each of you crucial allies in your individual and shared journeys of life design.

In reflection, building a supportive community might seem a formidable task—much like molding a life filled with intent and purpose. However, rest easy knowing that every step taken toward community development is simultaneously one towards fostering self-development. Every new connection, strengthened friendship, or enlightened conversation leads you further along your path. In this purpose-fueled journey of life design, remember the people you meet, stay open to new relationships, value your community, and cherish the magical web of connections that comprise it. Together, the journey becomes not only fulfilling but also an eminently heartening voyage.

# Chapter 11. Embracing Transformation: Reflecting on Your Journey towards a Life of Purpose

Embarking on the voyage of self-transformation, ultimately striving for a life of purpose and satisfaction, is akin to a caterpillar morphing into a butterfly. It is a metamorphosis marked not only by changes in your external reality but shifts within your inner self that are profound and everlasting. This chapter intends to pull back the curtain on the reality of embracing transformation, exploring how to gracefully accept these changes and reflect on your journey so far.

## 11.1. Change: The Only Constant

Who you were years ago, months ago, or even yesterday, might not necessarily align with who you are today—and that's perfectly okay. Change is at the heart of life's flux, and this resonates particularly intensely when you are engaged in purpose-driven living. The choices you've made, the values you've honed, the goals you've set—they're all pieces of an ever-evolving puzzle that maps out your existence.

In your journey, as in any expedition, you'll encounter mountains to ascend and valleys to traverse, rivers to cross, and vistas to soak in. Every new horizon is the result of a journey, every transformation a testament to your resilience and adaptability. Embrace each alteration, each turn of events, for they are integral to your growth and maturing.

## 11.2. Reflection: A Look in the Rearview Mirror

Reflection is a potent tool that offers context to your transformation. It illuminates the proverbial footprints left behind in your journey—the strides, the stumbles, the leaps, and the halts. Uninterrupted reflection allows you to trace back each step, each action taken in the quest to define your life's purpose. It offers a chance to appreciate the progress made, understand the lessons learned, and scrutinize the challenges faced.

Become engaged in a dialogue with your past, but do so with kindness and patience. Hold space for your triumphs amid the trials. Relay compassion to your past self who braved uncharted territories. When reflecting, remember that you did what you could with what you knew and had at that point in time.

## 11.3. Growing Through The Journey: A Conscious Evolution

Growth is not just about reaching new heights. It's about learning, engaging, adapting, and evolving—for every step forward in mapping your life's purpose is a symbol of personal evolution. The journey to a life of purpose is just as vital as the end goal itself, and it demands your presence, your conscious involvement.

Your growth through this journey is like foliage blooming through seasons. You begin as a bare sapling and gradually embrace changes—rain, sunshine, even storms—to burgeon into a thriving, robust tree. Each leaflet, branch, and bark is a testament to your resilience—and a promise of your potential.

# 11.4. Transformation: The Chrysalis of Fulfillment

True transformation—be it personal, professional or spiritual—isn't always comfortable or linear. At times, it may feel disconcerting as your old beliefs shatter, giving way to new perspectives. It may challenge your patience when progress seems slow or when the familiar morphs into the unknown. But, much like a chrysalis shields a transforming caterpillar, your commitment to this path, your willingness to identify and comprehend your core values, to design your intent-based goals, to balance your life—all serve as a cocoon enabling your metamorphosis.

Your transformation is a sign of your progress—each new aspect revealed is a symbol of your maturation. Embracing transformation, therefore, is not just about accepting changes; it's about welcoming your growth, your elevation to a higher state of being.

# 11.5. The Ripple Effect: Infusing Purpose into the World

The final testament to your transformation? The ripple effect it creates in your surroundings. Your purposeful life does not exist in a vacuum; it interacts and influences your environment. As you dwell in the realm of purposeful living, your actions, guided by intent, create ripples in the pond of your existence. These ripples, small or large, contribute to the world, imprinting it with your unique purpose and vision.

In the end, embracing transformation is all about honoring, cherishing, and respecting the journey you've made towards designing a life you love. Extend your compass of kindness and understanding towards yourself and take pride in each step taken, each hurdle cleared. As you progress on this path, let your transformation inspire others, light the way for those who seek to find their purpose. Your journey towards a life of purpose is unique, extraordinary, and completely your own—embrace it in all its magnificent glory!